Live It Great:

12 Real Life Lessons to Help You Create Your Own Happy and Meaningful Life as a Migrant

JOYCE ROA

Live It Great

12 Real Life Lessons to Help You Create Your Own Happy and Meaningful Life as a Migrant

ISBN # 978-0-473-43995-8

74 Sawyers Arms Road,
Northcote, Christchurch 8052
New Zealand

Cover design by Christos Angelidakis
Cover photo by Hester Roa
Internal design by Reynaldo de Guzman

www.JoyceRoa.com

To my Pogs,

coz where will I be if you didn't cook dinner?

DOWNLOAD THE AUDIOBOOK FREE!

Just to say thanks for purchasing my book, I would like to give you the Audiobook version 100% FREE!

(Check the back page for more details)

TABLE OF CONTENTS

FOREWORD

I LOVE THIS BOOK.

Joyce's words are simple yet penetrate the heart.

You will love her stories. How she met her one true love. How she stumbled upon happy miracles. How she became a tourist, then a migrant, then a tourist again, then migrant again. (Crazy.) How this gifted writer became a caregiver (or what they call a "bum cleaner"). How tears are turned to laughter. And how God continues to lead her every step.

If you're a migrant or overseas worker living outside your country, give yourself a special gift: Read Joyce Roa's book, *Live It Great*. It will refresh your soul. It will inspire you to live deeper, happier, and embrace this amazing thing called life.

Bo Sanchez
Bestselling Author

INTRODUCTION

Two tourists, one from Europe, the other from Canada, were talking over dinner in a holiday park dining room. The European said, "The roads here are crazy. It would say 100 kilometers per hour on one stretch, and then all of a sudden, it will be 30 kilometers per hour on the next bend."

The Canadian said, "Exactly! In my country, a 100-kilometer per hour stretch of road will get me to my destination right away. Here, who is the comedian who gave those directions? You can hardly run 100 kilometers per hour when there are so many twists and turns!"

These two visitors of New Zealand have learned what many other tourists had sooner or later found out; that Aotearoa, the Land of the Long White Cloud—or more fancifully, Middle Earth—has different kind of roads from other countries.

The popular paradise and the last bolt hole of many of the world's richest people, has roads with twists and turns that will sometimes make you suck in your breath, or make you a bit dizzy from the elevation. There are unpaved roads, and single-lane roads that allow only one car at a time to pass through.

Life, too, is like that. It can be filled with potholes, then a curve appears, and before you know it, another bend comes into sight.

It is not always possible to run full throttle. Sometimes, you can only muster a brisk walk. And sometimes, not even that.

You probably think your life now is the way it has to be. As a migrant, you have responsibilities to attend to and there's no way you can get out of them without ruining other lives. "You can't be a dreamer," you might say, "and still be able to feed your family."

Do you really want to live that way until you expire?

Or do you want to live a happy and meaningful life?

My last four years as a migrant in New Zealand has led me through ups and downs, highways and byways, narrow roads, and dead-ends. I came as a tourist, became a worker, and then became a tourist again, before becoming a worker again. You can say it's been quite a ride. Along the way, I have met many local people, other migrants, and tourists. Their stories, together with the things I have learned in the process of making a new life here, plus the lessons of the past, form the basis of this book and the simple great life that I want to share with you.

What is that life? Let me tell you a story.

One weekend, we decided to visit Milford Sound. We've heard it's one of the most beautiful places in the country and we wanted to spend our anniversary there.

Travelling through the area, I could see that it was true. We passed through thick forests where tall, leafy trees meet halfway across forming an arch over the road. We traveled on roads that ran along bubbling brooks, their delightful sound carrying through the air. High, snow-capped mountains stood guard over some areas we passed by.

Then, after a bend on the road, we came upon a burst of color—beautiful lupines in pink, purple, and white. A bridge split the beautiful fields of lupines in half. It was the most picturesque scene I've ever seen.

My husband stopped the car so we could take pictures. I, for my part, took a deep breath and stopped myself from saying, "Yeah, it's beautiful, but we have to keep going because there's a boat waiting to take us to see Milford Sound."

It was at that point that everything became clearer for me: Life is not about being a race car driver. It's not even that of a meandering tourist. At that point, I realized that life is one long pilgrimage. Every twist and turn, every unexpected bend in the road, both the sudden show of flowers and the end of a dead-end road, all are holy places that form pivotal parts of our journey.

So, in this book, I'd like to share with you twelve lessons that will give you a simple but great life through stories and insights. In lesson one, you'll learn about diving in. In lesson two, you'll read about how to open yourself to miracles. In lesson three, you'll hear how having a bring-it-on attitude can make the difference between living a life of pain or enjoying the ride. You'll learn about grace in lesson four. In lesson five, you'll walk through open doors. And in lesson six, you come to a truth: trusting in the Great Planner is the only way to go for a beautiful life. In lesson seven, you'll learn about gratitude. And in lesson eight, you'll look at giving of yourself. In lesson nine, you'll learn about living for real wealth. In lesson ten, you'll read about slowing down, and in lesson eleven, you'll learn the importance of being able to laugh. Finally, in lesson twelve, you'll hear about starting all over again. At the end of each lesson, you have a chance to personally apply the concepts in the lesson through some guide questions.

These are simple lessons. And more often than not, simple is really the wise thing to do. So, don't wait now. Turn the page! The lessons in this journey can transform your life.

Come on, let's get on with it!

LESSON ONE

Dive In Anyway

"This is as true in everyday life as it is in battle: we are given one life and the decision is ours whether to wait for circumstances to make up our mind, or whether to act, and in acting, to live."
(Omar N. Bradley)

A wedding. A red dress. And of course, a Facebook status update. That's how my love story goes, and how we came to New Zealand. The longer version is that I was a bridesmaid at my friend Jen's wedding. I wore a red dress. I caught the bridal bouquet when Jen tossed it and I was so excited that I posed for the camera, and posted the picture on Facebook.

My husband and I were already Facebook friends because we belonged to the same faith community. He saw my picture, was captivated by my smile (so he told me!) and decided to message me. We started communicating through Facebook, Yahoo Messenger (it was still the in thing then), text messages, and mobile calls. After a few months, we arranged to meet although we lived on different islands. It did not take long for us to fall in love, and after a few more months, we were married.

If our story was a fairy tale, it would have read "...And they lived happily ever after". It isn't as straightforward in real life though. You learn to adjust and then compromise regarding jobs, living arrangements, and other not-so-airy-fairy details.

In our case, it meant that I had to move to his area, and lose a big chunk of my regular income. It meant moving to the city—around 1.5 hours away from my husband's hometown –and starting a new branch of his travel business.

We decided to purchase a lot, and to be honest now, I don't know why we did it. After a short while, we also started paying for a house-and-lot. I was also paying off my own condo mortgage.

It was both a blissful and difficult time. It was beautiful because we were making a home together, and living as a newly-wed couple. Full of dreams and hopes, we were very excited and happy. After spending a lot of money renovating the place for our new business, our travel agency looked beautiful, fitted out in classy green and brown shades. We opened with a small gathering of friends and family with a priest to bless the premises, as well as some good food and high hopes.

Then came the trying months. We had hired a staff for the travel agency by then. The takings for the first month were well below our expectations. That's okay. Then the next month came, and the next. One or two months of those difficult months, we almost achieved our target income.

But then disaster struck—one of the city malls was bombed and our business was adversely affected. Meanwhile, our debts from the renovation and opening the premises were mounting; the interest on our loans kept on piling up.

One day, I picked up the mail from our front door; some of the envelopes were from our creditors. I sat down at our dining table and went through the letters. I looked at our mounting unpaid debts and my heart wrenched at my great desire to have them paid. I felt frustrated at how little we have to be able to answer to these responsibilities—and I cried. The burden and stress were too much to bear.

That's when we considered leaving our country to try to find greener pastures.

Were we afraid? Certainly. Unsure? Without a doubt. Were we excited? Indeed. Yes, we were all those things. But as we contemplated leaving the country and going to another one, we didn't actually just leave everything behind and hop on the next plane. We also planned. We prayed. We had consultations with immigration advisors from three different countries. We talked to friends and family who had lived or were living in the countries we were interested in, and we asked them about their experiences. We researched and researched. In the end, we made the jump and decided to go for New Zealand. That was four years ago!

What's Stopping You?

Perhaps you are a born-and-bred local and you cannot imagine ever leaving your country. Perhaps you never had to worry about finances, and you cannot relate. Perhaps the mere idea of changing the status quo tie you up in knots. Perhaps. But there was probably one moment in your life when you were torn between staying and moving forward, between the devil you know and the devil you don't, or between the status quo and the unknown. That's how it was for us back then.

There are moments in our lives when we have to make a choice. The choice is often difficult to make, because it will mean change in so many areas and the future so uncertain. But sometimes, the lack of finances forces you to make that choice. Perhaps what awaits you on the other side looks attractive enough to warrant a move. Or perhaps, all things considered, a move looks like the best decision to make. Whatever the reason, sometimes you have to make that decision. For you, what is it?

Life is not always cut and dried. Perfect conditions that all signal a green light on our plans may not always be evident. Options and uncertainties are usually the norm.

The key is that, after planning, you have to jump.

What's your own story to make? What's the choice that you're undecided about? What's stopping you in your own crossroad?

I'd like us to go through three possible reasons why you're undecided: fear, doubt and perfectionism.

Let's take it one by one. Fear. Who doesn't know fear, right? We fear and therefore we avoid. But instead of avoiding taking that next step, or making that decision because of fear, why not face or talk to your fear instead?

Fear is not necessarily an enemy, you see. Fear could also be a friend. Experts say that evolutionary biology has programmed us for fear to keep our family, tribe, or species from physical harm like a pride of lions, or a herd of elephants. Today, even though these conditions are hardly there, we still fear physical harm from the unknown.

Face Your Fear

So what can you do? Give yourself opportunity to face your fear—preferably in quiet—and see it for what it is beyond your emotions. Look at your fear like you would a cloud passing by. And then see whether logical flaws are present in your fear. If you are a Christian, ask the Lord to give you grace to face your fear. As the scripture says, "Love casts out all fear" (1 John 4:18).

Bask in God's love. Allow yourself to be embraced. And realize that though you are as dust, all your hairs are counted. Make your decision from that perspective, instead of from fear.

Doubt. Yes, we all face doubts at one point or another. After all, there are so many choices to make. So many options. It's good to study as much as you can about your options, but set a time limit yourself. "Okay, I will study about this plan to move for two months. Then, I need to make a decision," you can say to yourself. Otherwise, you'll be caught in analysis paralysis as I have been so many times in the past.

Perfectionism. Ah, there is that hydra. It seems so sedate, so proper, and so right. But don't be fooled. Perfectionism will kill your dreams. I know from experience. So just do your best and let it rest. As you've probably heard, it's not about perfection, it's about progress. You can only do so much, given certain conditions. The decision that you're making out of the condition that you're facing now is the best decision you can make. So decide and take that next step.

Should I move to a new house, a new city, a new country? Should I start a business? Have a child? Adopt a child? Should I study some more?

I don't know what choices you're facing. Whatever

it is, pray, plan, and dive in anyway. There is a time for calculations, for planning, for prayer. Then there is a time to let go, and to take action. You may fail, you may succeed; both are possibilities at the start of the journey. But you have to take that next step. Take that next call. Take whatever it is that will mean a decision and a moving forward. Sometimes a decision provides some level of certainty.

The Journey of Discovery

In the end, it's not really so much that you have perfect certainty or perfect clarity. The simple great life is not about that—it is about the discovery: the discovery of ourselves and of the Other, who walks with us. It is an ongoing process of discovery. It is learning, unlearning, and relearning.

Before I came to New Zealand, I worked fulltime for ten years in a lay religious organization. I wasn't a nun, but rather a lay missionary. During those years, I hardly watched TV or movies, and rarely went out. I went to daily Mass and had daily prayer time.

That was my life before I met my husband. So when we thought of going abroad, a part of me resisted the idea. During one of my prayer times, I realized that it was because I thought people in developed countries were godless materialists. Certainly untrue if you just use logic, but when you have lived for ten years in a closed environment that is so controlling that even having a haircut needs 'discernment' and where I was told people living 'in the world' are ungodly and not living God's will, my reaction would be considered normal.

But my perceptions were inaccurate. Through prayer, I learned to let go of my bigotry. After living in New Zealand for many years, I can say that some of the nicest 'salt of the earth' types I have met don't believe in God. The natural law is written in their hearts. So, I choose to respect them.

I let go of my idea of what is good, and just respect them, withholding judgment. I'm not a judge, and I'm not perfect. I don't have to sit on my pedestal. And that's good enough for me.

In the same manner, it is good to plan things; but realize that you cannot really plan for some things, such as your own attitude and others' response. Plan, but always be open to learning, unlearning and relearning.

In this chapter, we've learned to let go of fear, doubt, and perfectionism. And to approach the next big decision from a perspective of discovery, a willingness to learn, unlearn, and relearn.

Life sometimes feels like a tightrope walk between two equally scary choices. Hold the hand of the Other who never lets you go. Plan and then dive!

Don't worry; something will crop up, as our next chapter will show.

Personal Application:

What's your present crossroad?

What are your options?

What concrete steps can you take to research your options?

What are the pros and cons of your options?

A miracle can be unexpected outside help… It can also mean seeing another paradigm and enriching your view—as though seeing the orange in a rainbow for the first time.

LESSON TWO

Open Yourself to Miracles

There are only two ways to live your life. One is as though nothing is a miracle. The other is as though everything is a miracle.

(Anonymous)

My husband and I arrived in Christchurch at midday on a bright, sunny day in June. My husband's aunt was the only person we knew there, and she was supposed to pick us up at the airport at 6 PM. Since we had the whole day to ourselves, we decided to lug our bags, ride a bus, and check out the city.

When we arrived at the main bus exchange, it wasn't a bus exchange at all. It was just a row of covered bus stops where a lot of people were lining up for their various bus routes. The whole place –which was in the center of Christchurch —looked like something you'll see in a war torn country. It was my first glimpse into the devastating effect of the three earthquakes that hit the city.

We disembarked from the bus and decided to look for a place to check in our baggage. We went to their small information office and asked where we can find a baggage counter, and the staff there drew a map for us. As we were about to leave the building, two ladies with a young boy looked at us, and one of the ladies asked, "Are you Filipina?"

I said, "Yes, I am. Are you?" And they both said, "Yes," and asked, "What are you doing here?" We said that we were looking for a place to leave our bags. We explained that we were newcomers and we wanted to check out the city. One of the ladies then said, "Ah, really. Don't worry about it. We'll put your bags on the back of our car. Let's go and we'll have lunch." That lady – after living in the country for more than 20 years ––took a bus ride in Christchurch for the first time.

The second part of our New Zealand adventure had begun.

The Land of the Long White Cloud

Let me backtrack a little. We arrived in New Zealand on the 20th of March 2014. It was a beautiful autumn day and we were very, very excited to be in the country. It was the first time for both of us to be in Aotearoa, as the Maori calls New Zealand, or if translated to English means "the land of the long white cloud". We arrived in autumn, and since we were from a tropical country, we thought it was rather cold.

What I remember about our arrival in Auckland, was the cool toilet that would automatically open its pad container and emit a nice aroma. I know, right? Of all things to remember, that's the highlight! I also remember the flyers lined up in a corner. It was a lot of free flyers, a real eye candy for someone who loves to read.

We stayed in Auckland for a few days at a backpackers' place before we met with my husband's cousin. He brought us to their place which overlooked the city with its twinkling lights, a beautiful sight to behold at night. They treated us to a yummy meal. Later, we took in the usual tourist sites.

We moved to Hamilton after a few days and stayed with my cousin. We did all the touristy stuff, checking out the various places in Hamilton, Rotorua, and Tauranga. We checked out those places to see how we liked New Zealand and to decide if we would like to stay on.

We liked what we saw, but discovered that finding work wasn't easy at all. We just couldn't find work. Employers were looking for someone with local experience. As a newcomer, how can you gain local experience when nobody would give you a chance? So it was a chicken-

and-egg situation. Later, we learned there were jobs in Christchurch because of the rebuild, and that's how we came to the Garden City.

Miracle Upon Arrival

We met Jen and Noemi on that first day at the tourist information center. They took us out for lunch and then Jen's partner, Ben (not his real name), who worked with Housing New Zealand, showed us the various red zones of the city.

Christchurch had three earthquakes from 2010 and the last one, the most devastating one, was in 2011. Because of that, some areas in the city were declared red zones where you couldn't build new houses because of liquefaction. Ben showed us the various suburbs with houses totally or partially destroyed, and some looked as though they had been partly swallowed up by the land. It was depressing and discouraging.

Christchurch doesn't look like that now, and the central city looks more vibrant and alive, but back then, the place looked rather hopeless. But you know when you meet kindness—as we did—it balances things out. It warmed our hearts that there were people who were kind and friendly enough to welcome strangers. We felt embraced by the city.

And so, we stayed with my aunt-in-law for a few days. Her place was a bit out of the way and it was difficult to access public transport from there. We wanted to get around the city independently, so we decided to move closer to the city center. Jen helped us out by letting us stay in their boarding house in exchange for us funding their domestic tickets when they visit the Philippines, which they were planning to do. The deal enabled us to stay in the country longer.

On our first Sunday in Christchurch, we walked to the nearest church to attend Mass. After the service ended, one lady tapped me on the shoulder and asked, "Are you Filipina?" That's how we met Sol and Tim, a Filipina and Kiwi couple. They brought us to the country to meet Tim's family and to experience the Kiwi farm life—feeding chickens, tending sheep (and actually touching them!), crossing over a property line through a stile, wearing gumboots. Sol also introduced us to her choir mates and invited us to become part of the group.

Those first few days augured well for us. Those experiences enabled us to continue in spite the challenges, which eventually led to a breakthrough with my husband getting a job. That, in turn, enabled us to obtain a work visa, which allowed us to stay in the country.

Open Yourself

Life is not always easy, but experiences such as those that we'd had make me believe that if we open ourselves to it, miracles will find a way to enter our experience.

What is a miracle, then? A miracle can be unexpected outside help, like what happened to us. It can also mean seeing another paradigm and enriching your view—as though seeing the orange in a rainbow for the first time.

It is also understanding a situation or another person more thoroughly through an event, and thereby seeing a facet of a diamond that this person is.

Miracles can be as simple as being able to sleep soundly at night –if you have ever experienced difficulty sleeping, you will know what I mean! Or it can be as life-altering as those who have experienced near-misses, like the story of Richard's.[1]

A Near Miss

It was 1998, and Richard had just joined the Sacramento County Sheriff's Training Academy. As part of their training, they had to ride-along on a 12-hour shift with a deputy on duty. On the particular day that the shift schedule was posted, Richard was busy processing his vehicle insurance and he missed it. By the time he saw it, there was only one slot left—the South Sacramento day watch. He was disappointed, as he wanted to ride along with his cousin Danny who worked the night shift for the Sheriff's department. Richard had to settle for the day watch.

Richard rode with the deputy on duty, and in the course of their conversation, he found out their mothers knew each other. They also pursued and successfully apprehended a bank robber who had gotten away with money and Richard felt good.

Later, he learned that Danny –who was on duty alone that night – was involved in an accident while on a Code 3 Response call. On the way to responding to the call, a car suddenly backed out from a driveway and T-boned the police car, causing it to flip, jamming Danny's neck. He had to go on medical leave for some time. If Richard was in the car, he would have perished.

Richard felt special in the eyes of God, who had protected him from the accident. He had religion crammed down his throat when he was young and had no interaction with the church as an adult, except for a time the previous year when he courted a lady who 'lorded him out' by constantly talking about God. He remembered her again, revived his efforts, and finally wore her down. Today, they are happily married with three handsome boys. (You'll read about Iris' own story in the chapter on grace.)

Someone Greater

The topic of miracles can be rife for argument. Let's just simply say that it's an unexpected event that happens for the good of a person.

To be open to miracles is to be open to the Divine. It is saying yes to goodness, to mercy, to kindness, to saying yes to Someone greater than you are. Someone who fundamentally has your back. When you're open to that, life happens *for* you, and not just *to* you.

Being open to miracles also means letting go of your preconceived notions, letting go of full control, letting go of self-sufficiency and pride. Let me illustrate with a story of our Queenstown-Milford adventure.

It was our 3rd year wedding anniversary. At the last minute, my husband and I – together with two other friends – decided to spend the New Year in Queenstown. A crazy decision, because I had a friend who couldn't find accommodation back in October for their planned December visit. After scouring the web and calling hotels for a place to stay, I found us a campground in Kingston, 40 minutes away from Queenstown, and midway to Milford Sound. It sounded good, as we were scheduled for Milford Sound on the second day.

Our third day was supposed to be more tour of Queenstown, and then to spend our New Year festivities with the rest of the crowd –we'd heard it's the *it* place for New Year –, and afterward we'd go back to our accommodation, and travel back to Christchurch the next day.

When we arrived in Kingston, we realized the travel time between Kingston and Queenstown was too long. We decided to just stay in Kingston for two nights and chance our way in Queenstown for a place to stay.

While we were at the Skyline Gondola in Queenstown, I met a lady who worked there. She recognized me as being Filipina and we talked. I mentioned our predicament—being unable to find accommodation in Queenstown. Suddenly, without my prompting, she asked us to stay with her that night, saying that it would make her happy as she has a lot of food prepared but no one with whom she could share it. That New Year, we not only had all the food we wanted, and a proper bed to sleep in, but we also had a wonderful view of the breathtaking Lake Wakatipu as our backdrop.

Before this happened, I purposefully separated myself from my group. I was getting upset because we couldn't find a place to stay in. I was worried that with all the driving that my husband had to do, we would be overtaxing him if we just slept on the car—a very uncomfortable prospect. It led me to a point of desperate prayer. I had to let go of my guilt that we didn't prepare for the trip adequately. At that point, I just wanted to be rescued. And rescued indeed we were. So very kindly.

Do you want to become more open to miracles? Then become more desperate and more in need, and I don't mean just materially or physically. When you are desperate where it really counts–in the heart–then you become more open to miracles. And miracles can more easily come in.

To recap, in this chapter, we learned that anything that is for the good of a person can be considered a miracle. Being open to miracles means letting go of your adequacies and self-sufficiency so that you become more open to a higher power that has your back. In the next chapter, we will talk about a character attitude that you and I must develop if we want to live a great life.

Personal Application:

Do you think miracles still happen today?

What is your own miracle story?

How can you become 'more desperate'?

LESSON THREE

Have a Bring It on Attitude

"A pessimist sees the difficulty in every opportunity; an optimist sees the opportunity in every difficulty."
(Sir Winston Churchill)

Even at the tender age of eight, Chauncey could see opportunity in rice husks. While workers on her grandfather's farm winnowed rice, she'd gather discarded rice husks, sift through them, and sell those that still had grain inside. They sold for a measly amount, but she was happy anyway. Money was very tight growing up in a single income family, so Chauncey tried to bring her part.

She would gather water spinach leaves from the fish pond— while fending off huge leeches–behind her high school, and sell it to the parish priest. In college, Chauncey would sell stuffed toys her cousin had made to her friends and acquaintances.

Chauncey graduated band majorette and class valedictorian of her rural high school, and was able to finish nursing school through very difficult times. Her mother had to borrow money as her income as a teacher was not enough to support the family and still send Chauncey to school, and it involved many promissory notes and bitter tears. It never occurred to her to give up.

Later, as a nurse, she moved to the city and worked at a government hospital. There she brought her mother to be treated for her diabetic condition. Chauncey rescued her mother from certain death, rushing through several hospitals to find a cut down set (used to expose a vein) to save her mother's life from complications brought about by diabetes.

To save on cost, Chauncey was able to convince her own workplace to take on her mother's case, and she agreed to assist when they decided to amputate her gangrenous legs. She couldn't stand the sight of her own flesh and blood being 'hacked' down, and her senior forced her to scrub out. Afterwards, she worked hard to pay off the huge operation expenses they incurred, which she had borrowed from her second job. Chauncey held two jobs at that time. She would work from 11 PM to 7 AM at the hospital then from 9 AM to 2 PM at her second job at a diagnostic center.

She met her husband, fell in love and got married. Since Chauncey suffered from bilateral polycystic ovary syndrome, having a baby was a major undertaking, but even the risk of having thirteen hours of labor did not deter her from opting for natural birth. Today, she is a proud mother to three beautiful kids, wife to a man who loves her, and a successful manager.

She said, "Maybe the One Above looked down on me and said, 'Let's bless this pitiful child who has been working so hard, and that's how I achieved what I have now."[2]

Chauncey has the bring-it-on attitude, a quality that scientists say brings long life. To me, it just sounds like a boxer on a ring daring his opponent, "Okay, bring it on!"

But it's not really as simple as that, is it? What made Chauncey pursue her desire for a better life in spite of difficulties? What makes you work day in and out, toiling for many years? What leads a person to struggle on in a particular pursuit in spite the challenges?

Becoming a 'New' Person

I think it is this: They believe in what they are doing. Whatever their motivations are, they believe in whatever is driving them to go on.

When I think of my own uncertainty when we first arrived in New Zealand, I know now that I lacked this very attitude. I loved my life in my home country and hankered after my friends, my particular place in society there, my way of life.

Succeeding in your goals and dreams is similar to moving to a new country—you move from the known to the unknown.

It was autumn when we first arrived in New Zealand. My husband and I thought then it was terribly cold wherever we went. We quickly learned the importance of the bubble jacket, and made use of the item. Later, I learned about layering up, of having a camisole underneath to add to the warmth. Then there's making sure that my ears, neck, head, and hands are protected, because those are the first areas that I feel the cold. Then we also learned to have several layers of warm blankets on the bed so that I don't wake up in the middle of the night shivering with cold.

I also learned how to speak with harder Es so that Kiwis can understand me (a 'seven' should be pronounced 'seeven', for example). From a largely homogeneous place, I learned the importance of being blind to color. I also had to let go of my idea of what proper going out clothing was, since Kiwis have an eclectic and laidback attitude about clothing. For example, when you're in a mall, you might see a lady in formal clothes without any shoes on, or a man in an adult onesie with nary a second look from anyone.

New Wear

In the same manner, moving from where you are to where you want to go means donning on new wear, changing to a new 'person' that will enable you to adjust to new conditions. That may mean a change in the way you think, or in the way you respond to a given situation.

In my struggle to adjust, I learned the importance of having a bring it on attitude. Adjusting to a new life in a new place with new people can be very challenging. You can get discouraged, or depressed, and then eventually give up on life or on your dreams. Having that bring it on attitude means you keep that hope in your heart, and continue to light the fire of your dreams inside, never giving up even when life looks bleak.

You can scowl angrily at all the things that are happening in your life that seem out of your control. You can complain that life is not perfectly fine, or just not the way you want it to go… With a bring it on attitude, you choose to look at them and accept them as your present reality with no complaining. Does it mean no tears? No. But it does mean standing up after a good cry. It means resolve after discouragement. It means seeing the coming day in the middle of the night.

A bring it on attitude enables you to deal with reality more calmly, and gives you fuel to continue even with rough sailing ahead.

Rough sailing was Jun's life journey.

As Clear as the Sun

Jun grew up in poverty. His father died when he was just 10 years old and his mother had to take care of a brood of five children. As a high school student, Jun would wake up at 5:30 AM daily to walk for an hour, ride a small boat to cross a river and then ride a small bus –called a jeepney– for the last leg of his journey. Sometimes, in order not to pay the boat, Jun would jump off the boat before it could dock.

Many times, Jun didn't have any food to bring to school. Good thing he found another boy in a similar situation, and that person became his friend and companion during snack time. On school holidays, Jun would sell books, knocking door-to-door to find buyers. His summer earnings helped him fund his schooling.

For Jun, his goal was as clear as the sun in the sky: to finish college and get a good job. He did graduate college and planned to improve his situation by finding work abroad. Unfortunately for him, he was duped by an illegal recruiter the first time around, wasting precious money as placement fee that didn't go anywhere.

In spite of that, Jun persisted in his desire and was finally able to get a job as a school counselor in Thailand. The first few months were a real challenge, as he had to adjust to living in a new country, overcome the language barrier, and learn the ropes as an employee. But Jun never wavered in his dreams for himself and his family. Today, Jun is in a good place. He and his family have settled in their second country for more than a decade now. He has written a book that's helping others; his two children are healthy and growing well; and he's able to help more people through speaking opportunities where he shares his own journey.

In his growing up years, in the midst of all their financial difficulties and the burden of taking care of five children, their mother always encouraged them to go to church regularly and to have family worship time. Thinking back to those years, Jun's hardships are great reminders to him to be thankful to God who has always accompanied him, and to appreciate the present. Jun says he has two philosophies in life: "Never let anyone define your limits, and never stop learning".[3]

We have seen that a bring it on attitude is more than bravado. It is courage, persistence, and determination. It is having a sense of purpose towards the goal and dream that you are going after. It is also about adapting and changing. In the next chapter, we take up grace.

Personal Application:

Do you think you have the bring it on attitude?

What is your goal that requires a bring it on attitude presently?

How can you apply this characteristic to further your goal?

LESSON FOUR

Live On Grace

God answers the mess of life with one word: grace.
(Max Lucado)

As a sailor and slave trader, he lived in a culture where swearing was common. But John Newton cursed so badly that he was told off several times "for not only using the worst words the captain had ever heard, but creating new ones to exceed the limits of verbal debauchery".[4] John even wrote obscene poems and songs about the ship captain. His crewmates enjoyed them so much that they also joined in.

In 1748, a violent storm threatened the boat that they were in, which was sailing off the coast of County Donegal, Ireland. The storm was so strong that one crew member was swept overboard from the exact place where John had been moments before. They all worked many hours to try to save themselves, emptying water from the ship. On the 11th day of the storm, he was too tired to pump, so others tied him to the helm, and from one o'clock until midnight, John tried to hold the ship to its course.

Tied to the helm, John had time to think. He had been reading Thomas A. Kempis' *The Imitation of Christ,* and was struck by the phrase "the uncertain continuance of life". He also recalled the passage in Proverbs, "Because I have called and ye have refused ... I also will laugh at your calamity."[5] That day, March 21, 1748, John was converted. He never forgot that day.

John and his crewmates survived that terrible storm with the whole emaciated crew docking two weeks later in Lough Swilly, Ireland. Though he continued in slave trading for a while, his life was transformed, and John started a disciplined life of prayer, Bible study, and Christian reading. He felt called to ministry and eventually became a pastor. Later on, it led him to write the lyrics of what we now know as "Amazing Grace".

Grace. Such an ephemeral word. Almost like air, and just as important. Grace is defined as unwarranted or undeserved favor. And if we look at John's life, it's not difficult to conclude that he was not worthy. But looking at yourself, do you think you are worthy of God's mercy, of God's grace? Many of us would probably say, "No, I am not worthy." And perhaps that is the starting point of grace, that sense of poverty.

Daily Graces

But this is not a book that discusses a treatise on grace, for as author Philip Yancey said in his book, *What's So Amazing About Grace?* quoting E.B. White, grace is a bit like talking about humor, "Grace can be dissected, as a frog, but the thing dies in the process, and the innards are discouraging to any but the pure scientific mind."[6] And that's why you'll find that I am sharing experiences of grace, such as those that happened to me as my husband and I settled down to our day-to-day life in New Zealand.

From working as a manager in the Philippines, to becoming a checkout operator in my new country, then working as a caregiver while also moving house, I needed that grace very much.

Looking for a job in New Zealand was a trying and humbling experience. I initially recorded the jobs I applied for in an Excel spreadsheet but after a while, I gave up. The decline letters just depressed me.

After so many months, I finally got a job as a checkout operator in a neighboring supermarket and I settled down to working in a multi-racial company and became friends with some of my co-workers.

The job wasn't difficult though it can be challenging when you have to stand for several hours. I learned more about the Kiwi culture through my interaction with the customers and the staff. For example, I found that many, many Kiwis will visit the supermarket if we close the next day. We found it quite funny because we just close for one day and people will stock up like it's Armageddon. I also learned that just like everywhere else, the 24th of December is always panic time and it's best to avoid the supermarket then.

After two years of living in the same place, we decided to transfer house. My brother said to me once after they had moved house, "I will never relocate again!" Now I understand, and we didn't even move far, just to the next house.

I also changed job during that time, which was even more difficult for me. I became a health care assistant (caregiver). I cried buckets of tears during that job transfer. Part of me felt that all my education and experience were going down the drain.

Another part was crying due to loss of pride at working as a caregiver. After studying and working for so long as a writer, editor, and event manager, it was so humbling to start from scratch again—and many of my workmates had been at their jobs for more than 10 years!

Besides the physical work of dressing, washing, and showering a patient I had become a bum cleaner, as one Kiwi workmate laughingly labeled it. I had to memorize and report bowel motions and types (a necessary part of the job, since frequency and type indicate a patient's health). I also had to fix their beds. I had to do all of that within the space of three hours, before they have their lunch. With four to five patients assigned to each carer, it seems very easy to accomplish. But when you're talking aged care, even moving their hands or feet takes minutes rather than seconds, so it is challenging and time intensive.

The job change was so difficult because I wasn't sure if I was making the right decision. Was I doing God's will, or not? Was I pleasing Him, or not? What should I have done instead? All these questions led me to a time of discouragement, depression, and confusion.

Encouraging Words

What helped me through these struggles, were daily graces: a helpful work partner who took up the slack since I was so slow at my job; an encouraging word from my job trainer; the sympathetic and listening ear of my husband.

One time, I tuned in to a local Christian radio. The host was interviewing pastor and author John Ortberg. He was talking about his book, *All the Places to Go, How Will You Know?*[7]. John said, "We place emphasis nowadays on career advancement and reaching the top, but that's not how God looks at things. He looks at what you become due to your choices, to the work that you're doing". Those words really resonated with me, because I had thought about all my friends and batch mates who are already "somebody", while I was starting all over again in a new country.

My GP (general practitioner) said something when I shared about my struggle. She said, "Sometimes, you don't understand things. But later, you will. So just push on."

During choir practice, I chatted to our new assistant parish priest who came to watch us. He sometimes visited the retirement village where I worked to give Anointing of the Sick and to hold Mass for the patients there. I mentioned to him how much I was struggling with my new job.

And he said, "Oh, but they love you there. They love your smile."

"Huh, Father, how do you know?"

He answered, "Because I talk to them and they told me."

Grace came in the form of that sincere smile I gave the residents in the midst of my own pain.

Second Life

For Iris, grace came in the form of a second chance at life.

It was November 6, 2008, and Iris was having her

38th week prenatal appointment for her third child. It was also her birthday. The family had arrived in Italy on July 2008 –just a few months earlier —as part of her husband Richard's naval assignment. The doctor who performed her check-up said, "I'm not sending you home because you're already dilated."

So, she stayed in the hospital and asked her mother, who came to Italy to be with them during Iris' childbirth, to cancel the birthday party her mom had prepared. Isaiah came out so quickly that Iris didn't even have to push, and the doctor barely had time to catch him. Iris joked to Richard, "We should try for a girl next time, since giving birth is getting easier."

She was impatient to hold Isaiah and asked her doctor if she can hold him. But the doctor said that her uterus was not yet contracting and they were still cleaning the baby, so she wasn't allowed to hold him yet. Then she passed out.

Iris gave birth quickly, but her uterus would not contract so she continued bleeding. She was bleeding so profusely that they had to bring her to surgery immediately. She had lost so much blood that she used up the US Navy Hospital blood bank and they had to ask for more blood donations. Early morning of November 7, a radio announcement came out to the base families asking for blood. Around 300 people came out to donate.

To make the process quick and efficient, the doctors narrowed down the donations to those who were active duty personnel and recently checked. All in all, they used up 66 units of blood for Iris, and the doctors had to take out her uterus. Still at that time, she was only given 20 percent chance of surviving.

When she stopped hemorrhaging, Iris was transported to an Italian hospital, Ospedale Vittorio Emanuele, because the US Naval Hospital in Catania, Italy did not have intensive care unit capabilities.

Iris was put on medical coma at the intensive care unit. She saw her dad, who had died in 2005, and he said, "Come, Iris, come with me." And Iris told him, "No, Dad, I won't go with you. The kids are too young and I haven't even held Isaiah yet." So her dad let her go. Iris, who at that time was still in coma, felt something was obstructing her breathing. The nurses told her later that she pulled out her own intubation tube, which is a difficult thing to do. "She really wants to live," the nurses commented among themselves.

Iris woke up and thought she had just slept through the night. It was actually five days later. She couldn't understand what the nurses were saying, and she was totally naked except for a diaper wrapped around her. Thinking she might be in an Italian hospital, she racked her brain on what the Italian word for water is because she was thirsty. She only knew the Spanish word so she cried out for water, "Agua! Agua!" The nurse just answered, "No capito, Americana", which means, "I don't understand". Looking at the other five people lying in their own beds who looked worse than she did, Iris tried to figure out what could have possibly happened to her that brought her to intensive care. The Italian doctors and nurses struggled to explain what happened, and Iris got more and more scared.

"Americana! Miraculo!"

She called out for her source of comfort, "Biblia!" A nurse came back with water. "I asked for water and they didn't give me anything? And I asked for a Bible and they give me water? Well, you are Living Water, Lord, aren't you?" Iris thought. (Later she learned the Italian for drink is "bibita"—close enough.) The nurse allowed her just enough water to wet her lips then cleaned her up.

She was so scared that she was yelling for her husband and calling for her mom. She wasn't feeling well and she felt her life breath leaving her. At that point, she made negotiations with God, "God, let me live and I will serve you. I'm going to raise my kids to love you and we'll serve you." Still she could see her life flash before her. She repented of all her sins and felt God's holiness. She accepted that she was about to die and got excited about meeting God. Iris prayed for the Lord to take care of her husband, and that the two older boys will not blame Isaiah for her death. She closed her eyes and her life breath came out.

All of a sudden, Iris felt hope rise up. She felt like a balloon being inflated, given life by prayers from all over. Her eyes flew open and she gave a huge smile. *"Americana! Miraculo! Miraculo!"* the nurses shouted when they saw her.

Later Iris learned that she hemorrhaged and they had to open her and found out that her uterus was hemorrhaging so they took out her uterus then did another round of blood transfusion. They had sent Richard home to have a little rest but since she hemorrhaged, again they had to call him back. Her ovaries had hemorrhaged and they had to remove the ovaries as well.

Richard was told that Iris might still be out of it when he returns and that he shouldn't expect everything to be normal. So he came to the hospital that day worried about what it would mean for Iris mentally. He came in and she said to him, "You're off the hook. You owe me, Babe" giving the cutting sign. Before she had given birth, they had talked about his having vasectomy afterwards. Iris was able to refer to that discussion right away and Richard knew she was okay.

The Italian director of the hospital told them later, "We never really thought she will make it."

Iris did make it. Just three months later, in February, she was able to choreograph a dance. Today she says, "I have been given grace."[8]

In this chapter, we talked about grace, God's undeserved favor, which can come as small daily events or through persons or as major turning points in one's life. In the next one, we'll walk through open doors.

Personal Application:

What undeserved favor have you received lately?

What steps are you taking in response to the grace you've received?

"It is our little actions of faith, trust and generosity that shows to others that we believe there is a guiding Hand in our lives and He is the One opening doors for us."

LESSON FIVE

Walk Through Open Doors

When one door closes, another opens; but we often look so long and so regretfully upon the closed door that we do not see the one which has opened for us.
(Alexander Graham Bell)

Life is a great adventure, I believe. After a month as a caregiver, I had stopped crying and didn't feel too much like a chicken running around without its head. I could already tell what to look for when we enter a patient's room in the morning to sit him or her up for breakfast; I had learned how to use a standing hoist and a full hoist; and I had learned to bond with patients, with some even calling me their favorite.

Then by some miracle, a door that I had been trying to enter for a while suddenly opened. As an event manager in the Philippines, friends in New Zealand had told me

I should become a diversional therapist (DT). You work as an activities coordinator then progress to become a DT once you get your certificate. It involves planning and running daily and special activities for patients to help them in their psychological, emotional, spiritual, social and physical needs and well-being. (New Zealand has an aging population. By 2031, they expect that there will be over one million people who are 65 years old and above, or approximately one in five people.)

I had been trying to enter that industry but had been unsuccessful. But finally, after twists and turns, I was introduced to a unit coordinator looking for an activities coordinator. I applied and was able to get in. It's a beautiful and worthwhile job that's both emotionally draining and yet also fulfilling. I have been working as an activities coordinator for more than a year now.

Crossroad Reflections

I've gone through a number of crossroads that I had to pray and make a choice on what path to take. Do I continue to work as a checkout operator instead of going into caregiving? Do I continue as a caregiver instead of going into activities? Should I go into some other industry? These were all very confusing and troubling for me.

During the time that I was going through all these, the book *All the Places to Go* by John Ortberg helped me to ponder and reflect on my situation.

Some passages from the book struck me and helped me gain insights.

One passage goes, "When God brought the people of Israel into the Promised Land, he had them step into the Jordan first, then he parted the river." The Israelites had to exercise their faith first by stepping into the Jordan—then God gave them a miracle by parting the river. For my part, I had to step out of my comfort zone first by entering the aged care industry as a caregiver before a door opened for me.

This challenges our idea of having control. If you love having control ("I am the master of my fate; I am the captain of my soul"), then you'll have to rethink about that. The good thing is, the One in control is way, way better than you and me at navigating life for He knows the beginning and the end—and all the things in between too. You just need to give the reins to Him.

Another passage from the book said, "The open door is often more about where my insides are going than where my outsides are going." That was certainly true on my part. I wanted certainty on where God was leading me. I wanted to be sure that's why I was doubtful, afraid and confused. I stepped into a new door (in the form of a new job) still unsure. I realize I wanted a God who is like a traffic policeman and who would tell me, "You move forward. No, stop. Change direction. Turn left." I don't have a traffic policeman for a God. I have a father as my God—the most loving of fathers.

Uncertainty is a reality for migrants like me, especially when it's time to renew the visa, or something is going on in the country that makes our tenure unsure. Then our insides go churning like crazy.

I remember a lady I talked to who only had six months in her and her husband's visa to find a job and change their status to a more permanent one. She said she hardly slept for those six months. In fact, she took on two jobs since she said she would rather work than stay home and worry.

There's a song that I've been singing to our dear dementia patients, and they all can sing it even when they have forgotten so many things in their lives. The song? "He's Got the Whole World in His Hands." It's a good reminder so that your insides will settle whatever is happening outside.

Another passage from the book said, "Going through an open door always requires a spirit of generosity. And generosity flows out of an attitude of abundance, not an attitude of scarcity." If we thought the grass is greener where we are, then we would not move forward. We will hold on to what we have and not give an inch. But we believe there is something better and we can dare to be generous. We know something better is coming.

I think this particular passage from the book flows together with the other passages. The most basic truth they are all saying is that God is trustworthy and reliable. As we go through our open doors, we don't have to think only of ourselves, as the world always wants us to do. We should also look out for others, especially those who are in worse situations than we are. That is how we pay things forward.

It is our little actions of faith, trust and generosity that shows to others that we believe there is a guiding Hand in our lives and He is the One opening doors for us, even as we do our part to work the field.

Pushed Through the Door

For Dave, he went through his open doors because he felt he didn't have a choice.

Dave was 19 years old when he lost his dad. He inherited a bit of money and decided he could splurge. He went partying with friends, bought expensive items, and basically spent the money without too much thought. One day he woke up to the real possibility of going broke. He had been paying for his own college education through his share of his dad's money so he decided to do something to find income as soon as possible.

Since he was a nurse and many countries were looking for one, he and his friends applied to become healthcare assistants in New Zealand. They thought the healthcare assistant positions, which they had applied for, differed from that of being caregivers, which they didn't want.

So in January 2008, he arrived in Christchurch and enrolled in an English and Ace program (the Ace program would enable Dave to become a healthcare assistant). It was his first time to leave his family for a prolonged period. They were housed in a studio with only one bedroom, a lounge, and a kitchen. The women stayed in three bunk beds in the room while the men stayed in the lounge. Dave had the unenviable position of sleeping next to the microwave and waking up smelling like food. He also had to adjust to the cold weather, which he was much exposed to since at that time he didn't have a car yet.

They had no space for clothes, no cutlery and no utensils, though all those were included in their contract. It forced Dave to go to second hand shops and get some free rejects outside the shop, put them in his knapsack and ride the bus with the utensils making clanging noises during sudden stops. Their condition was later discovered and featured by one local newspaper which helped the government tighten procedures of agencies getting students from abroad.

After three months of study, Dave got work as an on call caregiver in Timaru, a two-hour drive from Christchurch. He was a caregiver in a hospital with regular patients and dementia patients. He would work from 11 PM to 7:30 AM, and prepared the residents' breakfast, mopped floors, removed lint from the big washer, showered residents, and folded clothes.

Another three months and his friends who were with him in Timaru had found jobs in Christchurch, and were thinking of hying off and leaving him alone. But he couldn't afford the apartment they were in if left alone so Dave decided to go back to Christchurch even without any prospects.

He redoubled his efforts at submitting his CVs when he reached the city. At that time, he almost lost hope. His previous job hadn't given him enough income as he was only called in if there was a shortage, and he didn't even get a chance to move around in Timaru as he was always on call. Now he has no work. But press on he did in spite the challenges.

A Turning Point

His break came when a friend of his called to let him know that one retirement village had accepted her but she has to pass it up. He hurriedly went to the village, and submitted his papers. Though he was second choice, he was able to get in. The tide had turned for Dave, though the next years weren't easy. He stayed in that job for four years where he became senior caregiver. During that time, he went home to marry his girlfriend, brought her to New Zealand and started their family.

There were many challenges for the new couple including juggling work and then going to school to become full-fledged nurses in the country, having children (they now have two) while both of them work, and for Dave especially, experiencing a crucial point in his schooling while his mom was dying. Good thing the school allowed him to go home to bury his mother.

In December 2013, Dave once again faced another open door when his senior stepped down and Dave was asked by the company he worked for to step up as unit coordinator for the dementia unit he worked in. At that point, he had ran the unit while the coordinator went on vacation. But he didn't want to accept the position because he had been working in the unit for just a few months and he felt uncomfortable at having to more extensively speak English to patients and their families. But he got his nurse degree under the company's scholarship program, which locked him to work in the company and his supervisors had said they had no other position to offer him. He either had to step up or ship out.

Dave decided to step up in spite all his fears. That was more than four years ago. Today he has come to his own in his work, being able to train other dementia unit coordinators from around the country when they first join the company. "The trials enabled me to know myself and to appreciate what I have," Dave said of his experiences.[9]

In this chapter, we learned that in going through our open doors we need to exercise our faith. We also need to check where our hearts and our emotions really are, to operate from a basis of trust. We also need an attitude of generosity and abundance. Turn the page and you'll read about the foundation to living a happy and meaningful life.

Personal Application:

What open door are you facing right now?

How are you strengthening your faith during this period?

What generous act can you do now to show an attitude of abundance?

"God always has something for you. A key for every problem, a light for every shadow, a relief for every sorrow, and a plan for every tomorrow."

LESSON SIX

Trust in the Great Planner

If God was faithful to you yesterday, you have reason to trust him for tomorrow.
(Woodrow Kroll)

For a short time, my husband and I were officially considered tourists in New Zealand. After three years in the Land of the Long White Cloud, we were back to being tourists.

You see, our work visa lapsed July of 2017. Although we submitted our papers a month before thinking that the lead time was enough, it turned out otherwise. I called the Immigration office on July 6 and the answering machine gave an ominous message: "Hello! Due to a more than expected volume of applicants, our processing time is now two months to six months." Uh-uh.

When I finally talked to a customer service assistant, the lady told me I don't even have a case officer yet!

So my husband and I became tourists. (This is an interim visa given by Immigration New Zealand that allows us to stay in the country legally until a decision is made. Depending on certain set of conditions, you could have an interim visa as a worker or as a tourist.) That meant that we couldn't work, and therefore we couldn't earn an income. The companies we worked in understood our predicament. They sent letters to Immigration to facilitate our papers coming out but they could only help so much. And that's why my village manager gave us two cartloads of groceries and some funds to tide us over. (We were on tourist visa for two months.) My unit manager also helped us by giving us grocery vouchers.

In a situation like this, it is natural to get worried and afraid, uncertain as the situation is. While I have been in that kind of frame of mind before, on this round, I had so much peace. I wondered how I could have so much peace.

In Mass one Sunday during that time, I heard a sermon that helped me. It's the story of St. Teresa of Avila as shared by our parish priest. St. Teresa is a well-known doctor and church mystic. She could spend hours unmoving in prayer, so enrapt in God. The sisters in her congregation asked her about it. Usually reluctant to talk about her experience of God, she said one day, "I pray the *Our Father*." The sisters were very much underwhelmed by her explanation. She added, "I pray the *Our Father* and I never get past the first two words." Then she added,

"The intellect has a place but first, when the soul is taken up with God, with the love of God, then it should rest in that." I had my explanation. I too rested in that.

An Ongoing Relationship

When I share here of trusting in a Great Planner, this is not blind trust. It is based on a relationship, a personal God who has shown Himself to be reliable, trustworthy and ever loving. It is based on past experiences where he has shown that he has your back 24/7. It is also based on years of doing your little part in this relationship, of starting each day with prayer; of learning Scripture and church traditions; of listening to him; of seeking time to be with him in prayer and in silence, or in music and in worship; of asking forgiveness.

Trusting in the Great Planner then means having an ongoing relationship with God.

Learning from the Past

In the past when I was fearful and restless, I felt as though my world was being rocked—as though I was caught in an earthquake. During my daily prayer times, I would be consumed in praying about these fears. The Lord made me understand then that He was my rock, the plateau that I could stand on securely. A vision of a tall mountain overlooking a lake or a sea appeared to me. I was standing on the flat part on top of that mountain. I could see what was happening around me. I was safe and secure, because I was standing on that plateau. The Lord made me understand that the ground I was standing on was Himself.

From that day, I knew that nothing can rock my world because He is my Sure Foundation.

Words from Scripture and inspirational quotes have helped encourage me. There is Jeremiah 29:11: "For I know the plans I have for you, declares the Lord, plans to prosper you and not to harm you, plans to give you hope and a future." Then there is a beautiful verse from Zephaniah 3:17: "The Lord your God is in your midst, a mighty one who will save; he will rejoice over you with gladness; he will quiet you by his love; he will exult over you with loud singing."

And, of course, this one: "No trial has overtaken you that is not faced by others. And God is faithful: He will not let you be tried beyond what you are able to bear, but with the trial he will also provide a way out so that you may be able to endure it" (1 Corinthians 10:13-15, NET).

Not Alone

It is not only that God is with us mentally, emotionally, or spiritually; I find that He is present with us as well through family and friends who love us and accept us unconditionally. Whatever trial you're undergoing, find comfort in knowing that you are not alone.

This chapter has been placed in the middle to say that trust in God runs through the whole theme of this book. If you don't have trust and you think it is every man for himself, you won't have a great life. It just cannot happen. You will be so busy covering all your bases that you won't have time to look out for others or to enjoy the journey. You just won't be able to rest.

It reminds me of many a team building activities where two people bond their hands together and catch a third group mate in the act of falling. It takes trust to just let yourself fall, unsure that someone will actually catch you. Remember this though: You are not alone. You are part of a team: God and you. Someone will always catch you.

There's a beautiful quote that says, "God always has something for you. A key for every problem, a light for every shadow, a relief for every sorrow, and a plan for every tomorrow." It's a good reminder in our own journey.

In this chapter, we read that trust in God is not blind; it is based on a relationship. And we learned that we are never alone, for we are part of a team. In the next chapter, we focus on gratitude.

Personal Application:

Do you think God is always near (Emmanuel—God with us) or somewhere on his high seat?

What steps can you take to improve your relationship with God?

Do you think you are part of a team?

How can you apply number 1 and number 3 in daily life?

LESSON SEVEN

Be Grateful

He is a wise man who does not grieve for the things which he has not, but rejoices for those which he has.
(Epictetus)

"Like all of us, she gets so busy concentrating on what she wants that she forgets to be happy for what she has." (Janice Kaplan, *The Gratitude Diaries*).

Raise your hands if that hit a nerve there. (Yes, mine is raised too.)

In a world that is moving so fast, gratitude is often taken for granted, overlooked, or downright forgotten. Instead of appreciating what we have, we often look at what we still need to accomplish.

And yet, we learned about gratitude almost as early as our first steps. Remember your mother or father telling you, "Say thank you"? By now, we should be experts at it, right? But sometimes, that may be the issue for us. Our concept of gratitude might be tied to our childish ideas of "I don't want to. I don't feel like it!" That is not the point here, because we are talking about intentional gratitude. This means that it's not about *feeling* grateful. It's *choosing* to be grateful.

There is a slew of studies about the advantages of being grateful. Studies have shown for example that regular gratitude can increase happiness by as much as 25 percent. It can make you healthier and more motivated. These findings bring home further the point in Scripture which says, "Give thanks in all circumstances for this is God's will for you in Christ Jesus" (1 Thessalonians 5:18). Sometimes our circumstances are less than what we desire, but it doesn't mean we should not be grateful. If we choose to be grateful, we'll have a better life of it.

'Stepping Out'

I remember when we were applying for our visa to be changed from tourist to work visa the first time around, it was a challenging time. We were never sure what the results would be. In the midst of that, I found comfort in the Don Moen song "God Will Make a Way". I would sing that song repeatedly in my mind, and then I'll say, "Thank you, Lord, that we have our work visa." I didn't see anything of course, nor did I know anything. I just stepped out in faith, as they say. It wasn't easy, but declaring victory rather than worrying of the negative helped me to settle. And yes, we did get our visa later.

Robin Sharma, who is considered one of the most influential leadership gurus in the world, regularly advises people to keep a gratitude journal. Many other well-known influencers do the same. And why not, when studies say having a gratitude journal improves your sleep and boosts your energy levels?

Your everyday life is good enough for a gratitude journal. My own gratitude journal is simple. One day, I wrote the following:

1) *Thankful for the day off, which gave me time to have a nap after lunch.*
2) *Happy that I was able to cook two viands tonight—stewed chicken with mushroom, and baked chicken with pesto.*
3) *Happy to be with my husband and that it's his day off work tomorrow.*

With that simple gratitude journal comes a whole new way of looking at life. They say that we are geared towards finding bad and dangerous things in our life (look at the news for one). Experts say it's because of our conditioning, which stemmed from when people were still living primitive lives and needed to look out for anything that would annihilate the family or tribe. That has been carried over so that even now we look at life that way even if we're not living on primitive times anymore. When we start having a gratitude journal, we imbibe a mindset of looking for the positive rather than the negative. In the process, as studies have found out, this way of thinking increases our happiness. That means lower levels of depression and stress, and therefore, longer life for the grateful person—the thing that our primitive ancestors wanted us to do in the first place.

As part of the grateful lifestyle, you can take time at night to name three events in your day that you are grateful for. As a slight variation from a gratitude journal, you can write your gratitude list on a small note instead, fold them and put them in a clear vase or jar.

The important thing in having a journal or taking time out to recall your grateful moments is that you don't mechanically write or say your gratitude list. You should really savor the feeling when you recall what you are grateful for.

Changing an Organization

I'd like to end with a story I read on Doug Conant. He is the former CEO of the Campbell Soup Company. When he came into the organization, he found the culture toxic. He said he wanted to focus on the things that were going well rather than those that were not. So he and a staff member would look out for news and happenings in the company that were worth appreciating. Every day for six days a week for the ten years he worked for Campbell, Conant would write ten to twenty handwritten thank-you notes. Throughout his tenure, he wrote more than 30,000 handwritten thank you notes to staffers and clients. When he came into the company, Campbell Soup's stock price was falling and it was the worst performer of all the major food companies in the world. By 2009, the company was ahead of the Standard and Poor's Food Group and its S&P 500.[10] Of course, you can't just ascribe the company's success to gratitude, but the notes Conant sent helped create a positive environment.

On a more personal note for him, Conant was involved in a serious car accident in 2009. He received get-well wishes from employees across the world. He reaped what he sowed.

Gratitude bears excellent fruit. Wise indeed are we if we sow its good seeds.

In this chapter, we learned that living a great life means choosing to be grateful. This way of life can be applied by 'stepping out' by thanking God even before you see your dreams fulfilled. It is also applied by having a gratitude journal or setting aside time to recall the events of the day. It is also showing appreciation to others. In the next chapter, we read about generosity.

Personal Application:

What three things are you grateful for today?

What concrete steps can you take in the coming days to grow in gratitude?

LESSON EIGHT

Give (of Yourself)

You have not lived today until you have done something for someone who can never repay you.

(John Bunyan)

Mely is one of our friends here in Christchurch. She is a feisty woman with a big heart whom many Filipino overseas workers consider their second mother. She has helped people in all sorts of predicaments and issues.

There was the group of men who were treated unfairly at work, complained about it, and lost their jobs. For many weeks, they couldn't find new work and needed financial support. Mely rallied friends and other people to give money or to provide food for them.

Then there was the woman who had a misunderstanding with her husband. Mely advised the woman, helping her negotiate the challenges of being married to someone from another culture.

Then there was the man who was brought into the tribunal because of drunk driving. Mely helped the man find a public attorney, and went with him to court sessions. Through the lawyer's help, the man was given a lenient sentence.

There are many other persons and groups that Mely has helped, including advocating the conditions of caregivers, of which she is one, and which led to better pay. She was part of the group that helped bring about the equality pay of caregivers in New Zealand.

Oftentimes, Mely does her work voluntarily and spends money out of her own pocket. Yes, she does that. And she will prepare yummy food in generous quantities for her friends, with no expectation of return.

Many people find many excuses for not giving—they're busy, they don't have enough money, whatever. But looking at Mely, I realize that generosity is not a question of money, time, or talent—it's a question of heart. Indeed, anything is possible for the willing heart .The unwilling heart, on the other hand, will always find an excuse. This reminds me of a story I read about giving.

Part of the Solution

It was 1933, and a family of four was on hard times with only one source of income; the mother worked as a dressmaker for others, but she became sick for a few weeks and couldn't work. As a result, the family couldn't pay their electricity so the electric company suspended the power and the gas company followed suit soon after. The water company was next, but thankfully, the Health Department made them turn the water back on for sanitation reasons.

The family barely had any food in their cupboard. One day, the younger sister came from school and announced, "We're supposed to bring something to school tomorrow to give to the poor."

The mother blurted out, "Poor? You couldn't find anyone poorer than us in this town!"

But the grandmother shushed her and said, "Eva, if you give that child the idea that she is 'poor folks' at her age, she will be 'poor folks' for the rest of her life. There is one jar of that homemade jelly left. She can take that." So the little girl happily went to school and brought the jam to class.

From that day, whenever the community faced a challenge, the young girl naturally assumed that she was supposed to be a part of the solution. [11]

That's the wonderful thing about generosity. When you give, you become part of the solution. Like that little girl, you are able to step away from your own problems and expand your horizon to include the need of others.

And when you feel that you are part of the solution, it absolutely helps you personally. Do you know that being generous is beneficial to your health? Volunteering has been found to be a most effective way of extending your life, for example. Isn't that amazing? When you give your time to others—in human terms, losing a precious commodity—by volunteering, you actually gain it back through an extended life.

You can't ever be more generous than God. You can never outgive Him. So while you may not think of living longer or any specific return when you give, whatever generosity you plant always returns to you. Indeed, you harvest what you sow.

Joining Humanity

My husband and I give a bit of our time through volunteer work at the local Society of St. Vincent de Paul. On Saturdays, we deliver food parcels to about three to five households that have requested for them in our given area by calling the SVDP hotline. We text and/or call them beforehand, set up a delivery time, pick up food that has been donated by churchgoers from our parish food pantry and go and deliver it to the families.

Sometimes, we meet one or two who are willing to engage with us in conversation. More often than not, they just want to get the parcel and get on with their lives. That's fine by me. I give them the most sincere smile, and ask, "How are you?" and if they don't open up, continue on my merry way. Very simple, really.

Something that I struggled with when I first started the work was thinking we're not actually changing anything. But there is a certain fulfillment in the work, and I was reminded of St. Therese of Lisieux who said in her autobiography *Story of a Soul*, "I had offered myself, for some time now, to the Child Jesus as his little plaything. I told him not to use me as a valuable toy children are content to look at but dare not touch, but to use me like a little ball of no value which he could throw on the ground, push with His foot, pierce, leave in a corner, or press to His heart if it pleased him."[12]

It reminds me that big work, small work, or no work –it doesn't matter. I make myself available to do God's bidding. It's His choice what kind of work He wants me to do.

Besides SVDP, our house is also the go-to place for musical practice or jamming sessions among my husband's music-loving friends. It's a good stress reliever for him and we get free live music in the process. Sometimes, my husband invites a friend who would record some songs, which allows him to tinker with the recording.

We also host a small prayer group in our house where we gather weekly to sing, pray, watch a teaching video from our founder, and share insights afterwards. And once a month or so, I edit and write for the local Philippine chaplaincy newsletter.

Myriad Returns

These are small things we do that have returned to us in myriad ways.

We have music and singing that removes our stress. We have had prayer and goodwill thrown our way just when we needed them, from friends as well as from others that we did not expect. We even have leftover food from time to time after one of these gatherings.

The great thing about giving is not that we have return of whatever investment we give. It is that in giving of ourselves to others, we see beyond our own misery, and step into the rest of humanity. And in doing so, we become part of what Michael Jackson sings in "Heal the World"–each of us becomes a healer and are making this world a better place.

That's the secret power of giving: it heals. It heals others—and it heals you. Because fundamentally, giving is loving. And there is no better cure than love.

We learned about generosity, which is fundamentally from the heart, in this chapter. Not only do we become part of the solution when we are generous and join the rest of humanity, we also heal ourselves as we heal others. In the next chapter, we look at living for real wealth.

Personal Application:

What are your passions and interests?

Who can benefit from your skill and talent now and can't pay you back?

What steps can you take to start giving of yourself?

"Being an eternal student and seeing everything around you as a child does--a world of discoverable wonder--encourages a sense of awe. It helps you realize that life is rich and wonderful.

LESSON NINE

Live for Real Wealth

"The real measure of your wealth is how much you'd be worth if you lost all your money."
(Unknown)

WE CELEBRATE LABOR DAY HERE IN NEW ZEALAND IN October. When I worked in retail, we had a lot of additional shifts that I could sign up for during Labor Day and other holidays. I could have chosen to work those shifts, but I didn't. My husband worked different days than me, and I chose to stay home and spend time with him. I probably shouldn't have stayed home if I just wanted to be practical about it, because the money would have helped us.

But I don't want to pursue just money. And running after money leaves you wanting anyway. Experts say that you just need to earn US$75,000 a year to have optimal happiness. Beyond that amount, you won't get any happier even if you earn more.

I want more than money. There's a quote that I believe is worth pursuing, "We believe that a rich person is not necessarily the one with a lot of money. It's the one who really has a lot to be grateful for; nature, the company of other people, the capacity to enjoy a good book, and an understanding of philosophy. The more things for which you develop a fondness, the richer the life you live." (*Thrive: Finding Happiness the Blue Zones Way* by Dan Buettner, page 56).

That's the wealth I want. A richness that moth and decay cannot destroy and thieves can't break in and steal.

Collecting Moments

As migrants, real wealth for us is especially about collecting precious moments with loved ones. It's not always an easy choice, especially if you live far and doing so would involve 'wasting' your time and money.

We were in New Zealand just one year when I learned my father was not well. He had become thinner, would hardly eat, and his second family feared that he won't last long. My husband and I had some savings, but we agreed that I'll just have to visit home by myself. My brother also came to visit from the United States, and we had a short family reunion. It felt good to go back to New Zealand seeing how happy my father was about seeing us.

Last year, my husband's father turned eighty. We could have chosen not to visit as we had just renewed our visa, but my husband is the only child and we had some savings, so we decided to go home. We were able to help in putting on a huge party in honor of my father-in-law, but just being there, seeing the smile on his otherwise usually serious face, was worth the effort we made.

What we did was not practical, financially speaking. But then, have you heard that the most often mentioned regret of those who are on their deathbed is because they have not spent as much time with their loved ones as they should have? Life is very short, even if days can seem so long.

This leads me to the practical side of real wealth. The premise here is that necessities have been catered to already. In short, loans have been paid, or are being paid regularly, and you have emergency funds.

Work for a Living

Living for real wealth also means giving of yourself to something you love. It can be as obscure as volunteering to open or maintain walking tracks, as I've seen among some people here do. Or it can be as mundane as volunteering for events as we do. It can be spending time writing for an organization, or it can be going out to play softball or rugby out on the field. It can also be baking for your loved ones.

If you are very busy, this might mean spending just a few minutes on your favorite hobby. These precious times are important, for they will invigorate you for the task of daily living –of giving of yourself to your loved ones.

Living for real wealth also means choosing to work for a living instead of living for work. This came as a lesson to me when we were new in the country. I have of course heard of work-life balance, and many people and companies seem to espouse these virtues, but actually make balancing work and life difficult.

But coming to New Zealand meant coming to a place that celebrates the concept of work-life balance in everyday life. It's just part of the general attitude of Kiwis. The general population is not out running after the latest gadget, or buying the trendiest clothes brand. I didn't feel embarrassed to say I want to go on vacation, because a fulltime employee is entitled to at least a month's vacation after a year of work. It was acceptable to go out promptly after work and do something else with your life. Kiwis generally don't define themselves by their work. It was a huge relief to step out of the rat race. Though I always used up my vacation time before, now I do so without feeling guilty about it.

I think of the quote from *Thrive* and realize what a rich life I live now: a kind and understanding husband who I can play and be serious with; a select number of friends who I can bare my soul to; family who loves and supports me; a job that is challenging and fulfilling; food on the table, and extras to share, and time to spare to help others who are in need. Not to mention to be living in one of the most beautiful places in the planet.

Eternal Student

Have you, like me, so often forgotten to look at your own front yard and to see how beautiful it is already? When you keep on looking at the small picture of your everyday problems and challenges, you can become blind to the fact that they are just a small percentage in an otherwise great life. So instead of just toiling and toiling, it's always good to step back—take time to pray daily, slow down and meditate, or take short vacations. Even if you just enjoy a few minutes of walking, or doing something totally unrelated to take your mind off of things. In doing so, you're able to distance yourself from the situation. You're able to see the big picture. You're able to see the forest and not just the trees.

Another thing that keeps that spirit of richness going is having a sense of curiosity. Being an eternal student and seeing everything around you as a child does—a world of discoverable wonder—encourages a sense of awe. It helps you realize that life is rich and wonderful. Albert Einstein is said to have retained this sense of wonder. He wrote to a friend, "People like you and me never grow old. We never cease to stand like curious children before the great mystery into which we were born."

The other key is to keep that sense of appreciation. A rich life stems from a wellspring of gratitude. A sense of entitlement will kill your sense of wealth very quickly, because you think you deserve what you have. Whereas viewing everything as a gift, then it is undeserved.

There is need for humility here, don't you think? It can be quite difficult to be both arrogant and retain our sense of gratitude.

Each of us faces different situations, and so will have to choose our own definition of committing to real wealth. The important thing is to make that choice; to make that commitment. The lyrics from the song "The Prize of My Life" encapsulates to the core of this idea of wealth. In just a few words, the lyrics remind us what real treasure you and I should be chasing after. For as Augustine says, "You have made us for yourself, O Lord, and our hearts are restless until they rest in you." When all is said and done, this is real wealth and true riches.

We learned in this chapter about living for real wealth, of 'wasting' time and money to grow our relationship. It is also about appreciating what we already have. Real wealth is also living a life of balance, of being able to pursue your interests and hobbies and to find fulfilling work. In the end, our real wealth is God Himself and our relationship with him. In the next chapter, we will talk about slowing down.

Personal Application:

How are you going to live for real wealth today?

Whom do you need to see or call today to 'waste' your time with?

What hobby or interest are you developing?

Learning to slow down also enables us to accept ourselves, with our strengths and weaknesses. An engine that is always running at top speed will soon retire to the junk yard. So it is with us humans.

LESSON TEN

Learn to Slow Down

Slow and steady wins the race.
(Aesop)

When we were new in the country, I would get up at the crack of dawn to prepare breakfast and a packed lunch for my husband. He had to leave early to catch the bus to start work at 7:30 AM. I would clean the house after he leaves, before going to my part-time job. At the end of the day, I would do more work at home.

I was happy doing it, but I had not realized that it was taking a toll on me. I had meltdowns when I would just cry out of exhaustion. Then there were bouts of flu that would confine me to bed for days.

I realized then that I'm not superwoman. And once again, I was reminded (through my body) what I had been confronted with one time in prayer when I was so busy with work: "What are you trying to prove? I already love you."

Looking at our world today, it is easy to realize that we need to slow down a bit. Notice how you react when a webpage is loading more slowly than you've expected? Do you remember the early days of computing when you needed to load a DOS disc to start working on a computer? We were quite happy with the slow speed of computers then. Actually, we were grateful there was a computer. If you are too young to relate to this, believe me, those days were super slow days of computing. But because so many things now are delivered almost instantaneously, our expectations of what is fast or slow has also gone up.

This lack of patience with slowness is all around us—the swerve to overtake a meandering grocery shopper; the impatient toot of the horn to a slow-moving vehicle; the setting aside of humans or technology that don't 'catch up' to speed (snail mail, anyone?)…

Looking at myself and us humans in general, I am wont to agree with what Larry Dossey in 1982 termed 'time-sickness', which is "the belief that time is getting away (...) and that you must pedal faster and faster to keep up."[12] In doing so, this affliction begs the question, "What are we running away from?" And conversely, "What are we running towards?"

Catching Your Breath

I remember those days when clock-watching was not considered a skill, and life was not driven by a to-do list—bygone days of childhood and youth when discovery was paramount, and joy was had by looking at shifting light for endless moments. Coming to New Zealand revived that interest to pause, inhale, and live for the moment, for the country and its people imbibe you with a certain unhurriedness. And then, of course, I started working with dementia patients in their 70s and 80s. Some of them would take up most of five minutes just to get up from a chair.

I learned to take a deep breath, backtrack from my a-mile-a-minute mindset, and look at life in a new way again.

In doing so, I've come to realize that catching your breath is good—not only good, but also wonderful. I learned to appreciate the fact that I'm actually alive, and I learned that slow breathing is the way to move from stressful thinking (and living) to wise living. The optimal process for slow breathing is six to eight full breaths per minute.

In slowing down, I've come to realize the value of meandering—of looking and appreciating beauty and simplicity and just living. I walk from the bus stop to my building through the retirement village, which is dotted with houses surrounded by gardens profuse with colors in all shades—yellow, pink, purple, white, and so much more! I could only breathe and thank God I have eyes to see and nose to smell.

Then there is perhaps the most important thing about slowing down, and that is growing your relationships. I remember the many times I've screeched to a semi-stop to walk a resident from one area of our lounge to another, taken a deep breath and remembered, "Wait, this is not a baggage I must cart off from one end to another. This is human." So I slow down, smile, and ask sincerely, "How are you today?"

In doing so, I get out of my world and into their world. I remember a line from the movie Red Sparrow, "Isn't that what love is—being seen? Being recognized?" In slowing down, you give yourself permission to really see the person and to 'fall in love' so to speak—to really appreciate.

Self-Acceptance

Learning to slow down also enables us to accept ourselves, with our strengths and weaknesses. An engine that is always running at top speed will soon retire to the junk yard. So it is with us humans.

Music has a beginning, middle, and an end. There are seasons for each year. There is summer, autumn, winter, and spring. There is a season for birth, childhood, adulthood, and getting old. That's just life, for life has a rhythm.

Slowing down is part of that rhythm. Learning to slow down is respecting a necessary part of life's rhythm—an aspect too often overlooked and yet filled with beauty.

Growing up, our house sat on top of a hill overlooking endless rice paddies. It was a fascinating sight to see their growth. The full-grown rice looked slim and sprightly in their yellow color, as the husks – weighed down with food ready for harvest – swayed in the wind.

And yet, to have reached that point, to have come up with that produce, the soil first had to go through weeks of fallow. During those times, all the rice had been harvested, and the barren plants would be left out in the sun to wither away. After a time of allowing the field to regain some of the nutrients, the farmer would plow the field again, turning the soil so that the richer layer would go up and he would irrigate the field with water.

Meanwhile, the seed is sown on special corners of the field that have just enough water to allow the seed to grow a little. When they are strong enough, they are transferred to the huge rice paddy where they are allowed to grow

–hopefully strong enough to withstand the onslaught of sun and wind and birds.

Richer Soil

You and I are that field too. As we respect the rhythm of the seasons of our lives, so too will we gain the fruits of fallow: a richer soil that is better able to bear fruit for ourselves and for our loved ones.

Let me close with a poem by Orin L. Crain, which he wrote in 1957, titled *Slow Me Down, Lord:*[13]

Slow me down, Lord!
Ease the pounding of my heart
By the quieting of my mind.
Steady my hurried pace
With a vision of the eternal reach of time.
Give me,
Amidst the confusion of my day,
The calmness of the everlasting hills.
Break the tensions of my nerves
With the soothing music of the singing streams
That live in my memory
Help me to know
The magical restoring power of sleep.
Teach me the art

Of taking minute vacations, of slowing down
To look at a flower,
To chat with an old friend or make a new one,
To pat a stray dog;
To watch a spider build a web;
To smile at a child;
Or to read a few lines from a good book.
Remind me each day
That the race is not always to the swift;
That there is more to life than increasing its speed.
Let me look upward into the branches of the towering oak
And know that it grew great and strong
Because it grew slowly and well.
Slow me down, Lord,
And inspire me to send my roots deep
Into the soil of life's enduring values
That I may grow toward the stars
Of my greater destiny.

In this chapter, we learned the importance of slowing down—of appreciating life and its simpler pleasures, of accepting ourselves and of growing our relationships. In the next chapter, we will talk about laughing.

Personal Application:

Do you sometimes feel that you're in a rat race, that you're always running and yet going nowhere?

What concrete steps can you take to help you slow down?

LESSON ELEVEN

Laugh

Against the assault of laughter, nothing can stand.
(Mark Twain)

Norman Cousins, an American political journalist had a sudden onset of ankylosing spondylitis, a painful collagen illness that rendered him immobile and at the worst of his illness, made him almost unable to move his jaw. Diagnosed as terminally ill in 1964, he was given six months to live. He was given a one in five hundred chances for recovery.

Cousins developed his own recovery program. He took massive doses of Vitamin C and had self-induced bouts of laughter through watching *Candid Camera* and other comic films such as that of Charlie Chaplin and the Marx Brothers. His condition steadily improved and he slowly regained the use of his limbs. Within six months, he was back on his feet and within two years, he was able to return to his fulltime job at the Saturday Review. Cousins lived another 20 years.

He said of laughter, "I made the joyous discovery that ten minutes of genuine belly laughter had an anesthetic effect and would give me at least two hours of pain-free sleep."[14]

Many of us believe that laughter has some curative powers. It's not that we don't know that laughter is good for us. After all, we feel that lightness after a good belly laugh. But sometimes, we get too serious about our particular situation. We become Atlases who carry the world on our shoulder and we forget we can actually put the weight down. I know because I'm guilty of this. But working with dementia patients has helped me get cured of 'seriousitis'.

Laughter as 'Weapon'

Dementia is a cruel disease for which there currently still has no cure. It affects the memory of the patient and normal daily functioning. For many, the past becomes more real. Some go back to thinking that they are a young mother, or a boss still handling their business, or even a young lady with dad and mom waiting for them at home. Generally, it affects people above 65 years old, though there are cases of early onset dementia.

However bad it gets though, I find dementia patients respond well to certain things. For one, a genuine smile coupled with a peaceable attitude calms them down. When you are lost and confused in a forever new environment, seeing a smile causes the anxiety butterflies to flutter down. I see it many times. This does not work all the time, but because experts quote "I may forget who you are, but I'll never forget how you made me feel", I follow this tenet with my residents.

The other 'weapon' that I use is laughter. Those in the early to middle stages of the disease (and sometimes, even in those who are in late stages), respond positively to laughter.

One time, I was reading a news article to the residents about a plan to chlorinate water in Christchurch. One of the residents asked what the use of chlorination is, and another staff responded that it's good for your teeth. The resident then responded, "What's the use when I have false teeth?" which made us all laugh so hard that we forgot our cares, if only for a short while.

In the morning, when I ask one of them, "How are you today?" and they respond with "How are you?" I then answer them, "As beautiful as you." That always brings a smile to their faces, a 'thank you' for some (with fluttering of eyes and even preening for one I know). For men, I'd say, "Oh beautiful, beautiful as the day", accompanied by a grin. That usually sets off some discussion or another. Sometimes, late in the day, I just muck around with the residents, dancing around with crazy steps in front of them. The smiles on their faces are well worth accessing my deeply buried inner child.

Working with these beautiful people who were once accomplished, independent, and led active lives, convinces me how necessary laughter is. For what is life if you cannot laugh? Even more, what is life if you will not laugh? For in laughter, we momentarily gain an upper hand on the forces that bring us down, and in the process, they lose their power.

When we laugh, we separate ourselves, even for a moment, from those things that burden us; of those responsibilities that we have to face; of pressures that push us –and not necessarily forward. And in laughter, we live for a moment, alive and unhampered—just being. It is a beautiful, free thing.

In this chapter, we learned that laughter can help us lighten challenging circumstances. We learned that it also enables us to gain an upper hand –even momentarily –to our trials.

Personal Application:

What concrete steps can you take to become more lighthearted towards life?

Go ahead, give yourself permission to laugh. Check out a YouTube video, recall a funny moment, do something.

Life can seem too huge and difficult to handle. But just the next step is manageable. That's actually all that is asked of us—just the next step. Just one small step.

LESSON TWELVE

Start All Over Again

Failure lies not in falling down. Failure lies in not getting up.
(Chinese Proverb)

IF YOU DON'T KNOW HIM, YOU WILL BE FORGIVEN FOR THINKING he is a ne'er-do-well. His partial history looks like this:

1816	His family was forced out of their home. He had to work to support them.
1818	His mother died.
1831	Failed in business.
1832	Ran for state legislature—and lost.
1832	Also lost his job. He wanted to go to law school, but couldn't get in.
1833	Borrowed some money from a friend to begin a business and by the end of the year he was bankrupt. He spent the next 17 years of his life paying off his debt.[15]

You do know the man, most everyone has probably heard of him. For in 1860, he was elected president of the United States. His name is Abraham Lincoln.

As you have probably heard before, the difference between success and failure is just one word: quitting. Your story is still ongoing. You can do a u-turn even on a dead-end, so it is with your life. Don't give up. And don't be afraid to start over again. Don't compare yourself to others. Life is not a sprint. It's a marathon. Define your own success and continue. Use your failures as stepping stones.

Starting all over again is a last step to a great life. It is a very important step. If you are like me, you've probably started a lot of exercise programs that died a natural death. You've probably read books that you didn't finish. You've probably started a hobby that you didn't continue. Some of these are a necessary part of life, of experimenting and learning and becoming better.

But there are some dreams that are crucial. You've probably dreamed of your own dream life. You want that life only to be caught up in everyday life, with that other life set aside or totally forgotten—just that, a dream. And remembered only with a pang when a song snatches you back to those dreams, or when a movie hearkens back to goals that never materialized.

Start Small

What is that dream that you have let go, that continues to draw you in? What is a goal that you know you could do if only you'll set aside a bit of time to accomplish it?

Perhaps you needed to first learn something more so that you could pick it up again in a new light, trying a different, more effective approach to achieve it

I was walking to work the other day and realized that my time in New Zealand has been a time of hibernation to growth. It has been a time of discovering new life after a period fraught with fear. It's been a time of discovering the new me after seeming to lose a part of me. Not really a new me, I realized, but a me that I had to pick up again after I thought the old me had died, and then incorporating the lessons that I have learned in this book.

So here's my take. Start over again. Start small but dream big.

Big is far too many times given so much air time. Big is praised, honored, and looked up to. But it doesn't have to be big. It doesn't have to be mighty. It doesn't have to be great by others' standards. It just has to be big enough for you.

I have shared with you 12 steps towards a great life. You might think they are too many and you're too busy. But how about you start small? Just focus on one area at a time.

Life can seem too huge and difficult to handle. But just the next step is manageable. That's actually all that is asked of us—just the next step. Just one small step.

As we step into each day armed with a sense of adventure, a willingness to open ourselves up to miracles, having the right attitude, living on grace, happy to walk through open doors (uncertain as it may seem), have the willingness to trust in the Great Planner, working on being grateful, giving of ourselves, living for real wealth, learning to slow down and rest, and finally—being able to laugh at ourselves in the midst of all our efforts, those small steps will spell a happy and meaningful life—a great life.

The journey always begins with the first step. Armed with the qualities discussed in this book, we should be more than equipped to take the next one. So what are you waiting for?

See you on the next bend on the road!

Personal Application:

What aspect in your life could do with a new beginning?

What small thing can you do to start again and live a better life?

ENDNOTES

[1]Online interview with Richard Eckles. 3 March 2018.

[2]Interview with Chauncey Gulay. 31 October 2017, Tagbilaran City, Bohol, Philippines.

[3]Interview with Jun Amparo based on his book *"OMG: OFW's Money Is Gone"*.

[4]"John Newton," Wikipedia: The Free Encyclopedia, 9 March 2018 <https://en.wikipedia.org/wiki/Amazing_Grace>

[5] "John Newton," Christianity Today, Christian History Section, 9 March 2018 < http://www.christianitytoday.com/history/people/pastorsandpreachers/john-newton.html>

[6]Philip Yancey, What's So Amazing About Grace? (Zondervan, Grand Rapids, Michigan, 1997) 16.

[7]John Ortberg, All the Places to Go…How Will You Know?: God Has Placed Before You an Open Door. What Will You Do? (Tyndale House Publishers, Inc., 2015).

[8] Online interview with Iris Eckles. 27 February 2018.

[9]Interview with Dave Sevilleno. 2 March 2018, Christchurch, New Zealand.

[10]Shana Lebowitz, "How the Former CEO of Campbell Soup Used a Skill Taught in Kindergarten to Motivate His Entire Company", Business Insider Australia, 10 March 2017 <https://www.businessinsider.com.au/why-leaders-should-show-gratitude-to-their-employees-2016-11?r=US&IR=T>

[11]"Out of a Jam" by Edgar Bledsoe, A Cup of Chicken Soup for the Soul (Health Communications, Inc, 1996) 68.

[12]John Clarke, OCD, Story of a Soul: The Autobiography of St. Therese of Lisieux (the Little Flower) [The Authorized English Translation of Therese's Original Unaltered Manuscripts] (ICS Publications, 1996) 136.

[12]Quoted in "Slowing Down in an Age of Speed", Homaira Kabir, Positive Psychology News, 10 March 2018 <http://positivepsychologynews.com/news/homaira-kabir/2015090734815>

[13] "Slow Me Down, Lord" as quoted from Beth Armstrong blog, 10 March 2018 https://mbetharmstrong.wordpress.com/2013/07/08/slow-me-down-lord/>.

[14] "Norman Cousins," Wikipedia: The Free Encyclopedia, 9 March 2018 <https://en.wikipedia.org/wiki/Norman_Cousins>

[15] "Abraham Lincoln Didn't Quit" by source unknown, Chicken Soup for the Soul (Health Communications, Inc, 1993) 236.

ACKNOWLEDGMENT

This book had a journey of its own before it became a reality. I would like to thank the following for making this project possible:

- My husband Hester who has always supported me in my endeavors. I still get teary-eyed when I remember you saying 'yes' to my joining Self-Publishing School (SPS) so I can make my dream of writing a book a reality by following a step-by-step process. Then there were the many nights you cooked dinner; the many times I ignored you, lost in my own world; the times you've read my work and encouraged me, not to mention being my photographer, audio recorder, marketer, etc. For these and the myriad of ways you have loved me, thank you! I love you, Honey!

- To my brother from the same mother Jojo who has been asking me to write a book for the longest time, you will always be more precious than gold to me—thank you! And thank you too, Brenda, for always loving and supporting me along with Jojo.

And you boys Dave and Z (I know you are men now, but you'll always be boys to me), this is not quite Snapchat so you can read this book slowly. It won't disappear the next day. I am hoping to leave a better world for you both.

- To Ate Mely, Ate Ludy and Kat—your friendship means a lot to me. Sounding board, travel buddies, crazy mates, prayer companions and everything else—what else can I ask for?

- To Papa Okie, Papa Cancio and Mama Emma—thank you for feeding us, encouraging us, challenging us. Thank you for everything!

- To Junjun and Jho; to Cielo and family; to Ate Elena, Anthony and family—thank you for your continuing support, encouragement and friendship. You were our first faces of New Zealand, and yours were generous and beautiful ones!

- To Self-Publishing School, especially to Chandler Bolt and Sean Sumner, and the many members who guided, encouraged and inspired me to finish this book—thank you! And a special thanks to my coach, Lise Cartwright, for making it easier for me to traverse the road to self-publishing through her guidance and encouragement.

- To my accountability partner Margaret Butler for helping me along through her own journey and her encouraging words.

- To these friends and beta readers Dina Pecana, Tess Atienza, Sylvia Pierce and Iris Eckles—thank you for your feedback and encouragement. They were invaluable!

- To Anna Santos for journeying with me in writing, coaching and living as a migrant.

- To these special people: Richard and Iris Eckles, Jun Amparo, Chauncey Gulay, Dave and Amor Sevilleno—thank you for sharing your stories! You have encouraged me tremendously. May this book help spread that encouragement to others.

- To Ate Chelle Crisanto—you will always be my exemplar of the *it* lady: fun, fashionable and faithful. Thank you!
- To Maricel and Holger Weischede—your guidance and friendship continue to help us in our migrant

journey—thank you!

- To the members of the Our Lady of Fatima Catholic Choir—thank you! We wouldn't have settled so well in Christchurch if not for your kindness and friendship. Special thanks to Ate Arlene Wilkins who's such a patient and considerate leader in the choir and in the chaplaincy.

- To my editor Lizette Balsdon; my book cover artist Christos Angelidakis; and my book formatter Kuya Rey de Guzman; my audiobook engineer Roly Chris Cosing—I wouldn't have been able to finish this project without your crucial assistance.

- To my mentors: John Assaraf for helping me overcome my self-limiting beliefs and for showing me a personal and warm example of online presence; and, for Joanna Penn for 'being there' all the time through these many years before officially becoming an author—your podcast, blog, video, tweets and books shed much needed light throughout the journey.

- To Bo Sanchez, my mentor in writing, in life, and in business—you are God's gift indeed! Thank you seems inadequate but I hope a little of what I do adds to the light that you spread.

- And to the Beginning and the End; my Muse, my Inspiration, my Rock and my Hiding Place—this is for You. I love you, Lord!

DOWNLOAD THE AUDIOBOOK FREE!

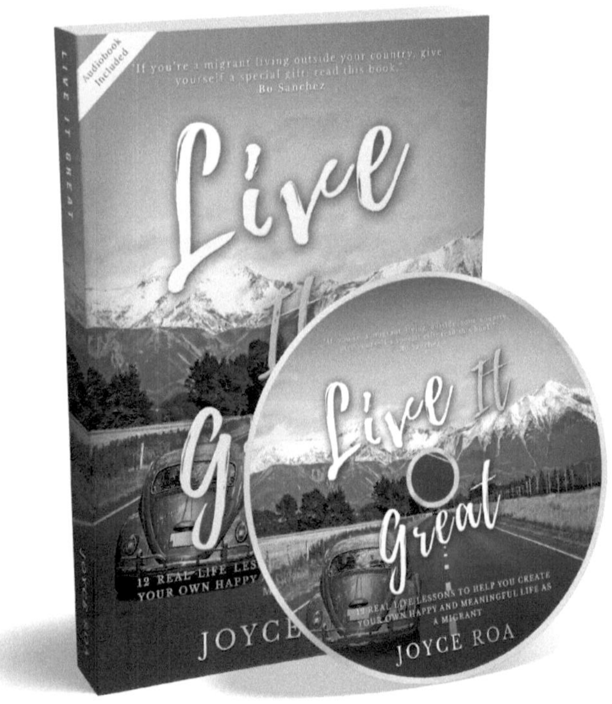

You can download the audiobook version here:
https://mailchi.mp/joyceroa.com/liveitgreataudiobook

Thank You for Downloading My Book!

I really appreciate your feedback, and
I love hearing what you have to say.
If you liked this book, please consider leaving a helpful review on Amazon. It will help others discover the book.
Thanks so much!

– Joyce Roa

Live It Great

www.ingramcontent.com/pod-product-compliance
Ingram Content Group UK Ltd.
Pitfield, Milton Keynes, MK11 3LW, UK
UKHW042015190726
13854UKWH00005B/2291